Victoria~

Cock

and Other ~ories

*Clearly, Vanessa's new vibrator would never
fit into her handbag.*

Written and Compiled by
The Very Rev'd Stephen Lovering LLD (Oxon)

Published by McNaughty Books, an imprint of John Napir Ltd

P.O.Box 3353. London N1 1SR

ISBN 1-898505-608

Printed and bound in the U.K.

Contents

Though successful, Lydia's acne ointment had
one slight side effect.

Chapter 1

Victorian Cock-ups

by

The Very Rev'd Stephen Lovering LLD (Oxon)

Despite being craftsman-built to a rigorous
standard, the Perry brothers sex doll was
doomed to failure.

Suddenly Julia decided to bite off the
Major's goolies.

Clearly, Vanessa's new vibrator would never fit
into her handbag.

Though successful, Barry's experimental
trouser-press ruined his wedding plans.

Clearly, Rupert's new marital aid required
further research and development.

Edward's parents desperately hoped
cycle-humping was a phase he'd soon grow
out of.

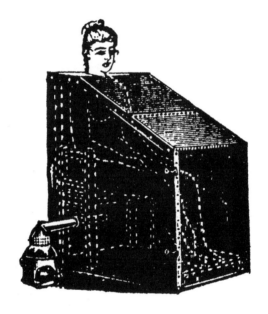

Its efficiency as a contraceptive device far
outweighed its lack of mobility

Chapter 2

This Sporting Life

by

Hubert Nutless-Hurdler Esq

Finally the referee gave them just three
minutes to agree on the game.

Proudly Ernest demonstrated the art of
formation gnat flying.

"That's nothing", Cruella smirked, "yesterday I caught one this big".

The next time Gladys entered the cage she was
better prepared.

Levi's were first tested during Tom Brown's
schooldays.

That year the Prussian formation diving team
swept the board.

Once more, Monty's arm wrestling brought
tears to his grandfathers eyes.

Sadly, it was the invisible man's last attempt at
weightlifting.

That day, Lionel began training as a delivery
boy at the William Tell Pizza Academy.

Chapter 3

A Jolly Good Nosh

by
Miss Whiney Michael & Ronny Egon

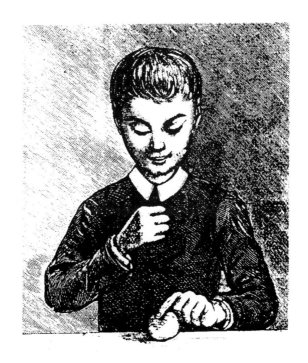

In no time at all Josh had rolled a giant bogie ball.

Marco had no time for restaurant critics.

The next time Adam and Eve really copped the
Wrath of God.

Hercules' final task was delivering take-away
tandoori in Southall.

This time, Gregory's Jerry Lee Lewis
Impersonations ended in tears.

Chapter 4

Music Hall Merriment and Beyond

by
Snotti Castrati and his Flying Slugs

In heaven, Hendrix was able to broaden his
artistic pursuits.

His costume complete, Giles now had only to
master the Ken Dodd Joke Book.

Rudolph's passion for the tango ceased the day
his partner wore a gown trimmed with his
Uncle Frank.

Brian's synchronised window cleaners failed to
arouse the audience.

Miranda quickly adapted her ventriloquist act
to suit the Luton Nudist Club cabaret.

Lucy couldn't persuade the Peeing Boy of
Brussels to give an impromptu performance.

Once again Quigley's musical farting had
failed to amuse the lower third.

Chapter 5

Fragrant Fashions

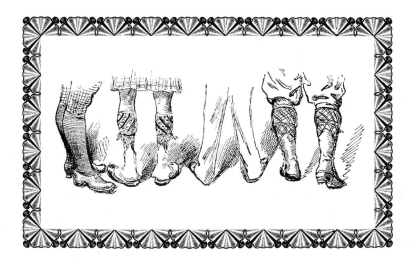

by
Mrs Flavia Dollymop

At 14, Wendy was concerned about her
underdeveloped bustle.

Then all of a sudden Alice took to wearing a
cricket box.

Reluctantly, Miranda agreed to part company
with Weight Watchers.

Wayne had despaired of flairs ever making a
come-back, when there was a knock at the
door.

Stubbornly, Beatrice insisted on wearing her
Bonsai to the Christmas Party.

Not for the first time, Reg felt uncomfortably overdressed.

Julia thanked her lucky stars that her diet was now behind her.

Mrs Gulliver was the toast of Royal Ascot.

Caught once more in drag, Tinkerbell fidgeted
nervously.

Chapter 6

Gay Times

by
Sebastian Tail-Buzzer Esq

That spring Edward began acting strangely.

The "Playboy Tenors in Hot Pants" calendar
failed to arouse much interest.

For the third year running Bill was crowned
Biggelswade Drag Queen.

The other boys wondered if Barnaby would ever
come out.

Miranda's pile treatment was an astonishing
success.

Chapter 7

Modern Medicine Explained

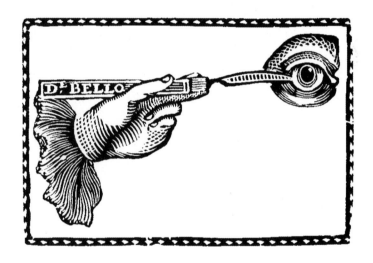

by
Dr Horatio Pillbocks

Then Marcia knitted her own tonsils.

Walter jubilantly carried off the first prize in
the Medical School raffle.

Dr Condom's prototypes may have caused
some discomfort.

What I prescribe, Mrs Pankhurst, is a jolly
good rogering.

Back then varicose veins were considered
highly fashionable.

Since his operation, Ralph's party piece was to
lasso his top hat with his small intestine.

In those days, a fortnight in Eastbourne was
the only treatment for cauliflower ears.

Dr Zukhof's cure for bedwetting was cruel but
effective.

What's more, Ralph was prepared to
demonstrate that every part of him was in
perfect proportion.

Dereck demonstrated his unique cure for nose picking.

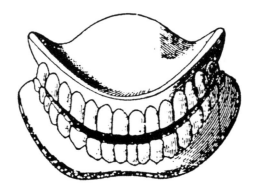

His formula 99% effective, the invisible man
smiled triumphantly.

Chapter 8

Recent Scientific
Developments

by
Prof Reiner von Deisel MSc B.F Q.V Etc

Gustave was an avid enthusiast of in-car
entertainment.

In the end poor technology defeated the
Melbourne to London tunnel.

Thereafter sales of Benchly's Maritime Power
Shower slumped dramatically.

"And every one grown from seed" Ngooma said
proudly.

Never again did Roger borrow Leo's
underpants.

Chapter 9

War and other Necessary Disasters

by
Major Sir Norman John V.C. (Retired)

Suddenly Larry's maraca-playing ignited
Maureen's bustle.

At that moment a passing pigeon relieved
itself.

Nervously, Zelda outlined the Zoo's
redundancy package.

From the start Leon's dual was a one-sided affair.

The gruesome remains of the Bronte sisters
were then revealed to the Court.

Finally the Government found a sponsor for its gunboat policy.

The forecast was right, a small plague of frogs
around lunchtime.

McNaughty
Books

McNAUGHTY BOOKS	£
The McNaughty Book of Limericks by Farquhar McNaughty	**4.99**
The McIrish Book of Logic by Seamus O'Really	**4.99**
The McVeggie Book of Rude Food by Squirty O'Gourd	**4.99**
The McTory Book of Bonks by Norman ffamily-Values	**4.99**
Victorian Cock-Ups and Other Stories by The Very Rev'd Steve Lovering	**4.99**
How to be a Politically Correct Sex Maniac by Johnny Condom	**4.99**
The Little Sexpot's Instruction Book	**3.99**

McNaughty Books are available from all good Book and Gift shops, or direct from the publishers John Napir Ltd. at P.O. Box 3353, London N1.

Suddenly, Raymond remembered he'd left the bath running.